Denver Nuggets Epic History

Epic History

Published by Epic History, 2024.

DENVER NUGGETS EPIC HISTORY

First edition. February 29, 2024.

ISBN: 979-8224202362

Written by Epic History.

Also by Epic History

New Jersey Devils Epic History
Detroit Red Wings Epic History
Denver Nuggets Epic History

Table of Contents

Denver Nuggets Epic History

The Mile High Legacy: A Comprehensive History of the Denver Nuggets from Inception to Present Day

The Denver Nuggets have a storied history that dates back to their inception in 1967 as the charter franchise of the American Basketball Association (ABA). Throughout the decades, this team has showcased a commitment to excellence and passion for basketball that has endeared them to fans nationwide. From their early struggles in the ABA era to their transition into the NBA in 1976, and finally reaching new heights with consecutive playoff appearances in recent years, the Denver Nuggets have left an indelible mark on professional basketball. Join us on a journey through time as we explore the Mile High Legacy of the Denver Nuggets, highlighting key moments, iconic players, memorable games, and pivotal decisions that have shaped this beloved franchise into what it is today.

The Birth of the Denver Nuggets: A Look at the ABA Era

1. In 1967, the Denver Nuggets were born as a franchise in the American Basketball Association (ABA), joining seven other teams in this up-and-coming league.
2. The team quickly made an impact with their fast-paced style of play and high-scoring offense, becoming known for their exciting brand of basketball.
3. During their time in the ABA, the Nuggets experienced success on the court, making it to the playoffs multiple times and solidifying themselves as a force to be reckoned with in professional basketball.

The Move to the NBA: Challenges and Triumphs

When the Denver Nuggets made the transition from the ABA to the NBA in 1976, they faced a variety of challenges. They had to adjust to a new level of competition and deal with financial constraints that came with joining a larger league. Despite these obstacles, the Nuggets quickly proved themselves on the court, showcasing their talent and determination.

One of their early triumphs in the NBA was reaching the playoffs in their inaugural season. Led by star player David Thompson, they made a statement by making it all the way to the conference finals. This success helped establish them as a force to be reckoned with in the league and set them on course for future achievements.

Mile High Basketball: The Nuggets' Impact on Denver

Since their founding in 1967, the Denver Nuggets have become an integral part of the city's sports culture. With a passionate fan base and a history of exciting playoff runs, the Nuggets have left a lasting impact on Denver.

● The team has showcased top talent over the years, including legendary players like Alex English and Carmelo Anthony.

● Their high-flying style of play has earned them the nickname "Runnin' Nuggets" and created memorable moments for fans.

● Through community outreach programs and charity events, the Nuggets have shown a commitment to giving back to the city that supports them.

Overall, the Denver Nuggets continue to be a source of pride for residents and demonstrate how basketball can bring people together in support of a common goal.

The Alex English Era: A Golden Age for the Nuggets

- In the 1980s, the Denver Nuggets experienced a period of unparalleled success under the leadership of Hall of Famer Alex English.

- Known for his smooth shooting touch and scoring prowess, English became the face of the franchise during this golden age.

- With English leading the way, the Nuggets made multiple playoff appearances and captivated fans with their high-octane style of play.

During this era:

1. Alex English consistently ranked among the league's top scorers, earning eight All-Star selections.
2. The team's up-tempo offense earned them a reputation as one of the most exciting teams to watch in the NBA.
3. Despite falling short of an NBA championship, English's impact on and off court cemented his legacy as one of Denver's all-time greats.

A Rocky Road: The Nuggets' Struggles in the 1990s

- The Denver Nuggets faced numerous challenges during the 1990s, leading to a period of struggle for the team.

- Despite having talented players like Dikembe Mutombo and Mahmoud Abdul-Rauf, the Nuggets failed to make a significant impact in the NBA.

- Injuries, inconsistent performances, and management issues plagued the team throughout this decade.

Rebuilding Efforts and Hope for the Future

- As the 1990s came to a close, the Denver Nuggets began rebuilding their roster through smart draft picks and strategic acquisitions.

- This renewed focus on player development laid the foundation for future success for the franchise.

- Fans remained hopeful that better days were ahead for their beloved team.

The Carmelo Anthony Years: Playoff Success and Controversy

- **Playoff Success**: During his time with the Denver Nuggets, Carmelo Anthony led the team to multiple playoff appearances, showcasing his scoring prowess and leadership on the court. In the 2008-2009 season, he guided the Nuggets to the Western Conference Finals for the first time in nearly two decades.

- **Off-Court Controversy**: However, Anthony's tenure in Denver was not without controversy. His desire to be traded amid contract negotiations created tension within the organization and among fans. Ultimately, he was dealt to the New York Knicks in a blockbuster trade that reshaped both franchises.

Despite mixed feelings about his departure, Carmelo Anthony's impact on the Denver Nuggets franchise cannot be overstated. His scoring ability and playoff success helped revive a struggling team and bring it back into championship contention during his time with them. While there were ups and downs along the way, there is no denying that Anthony left a lasting legacy in Mile High City before moving on to continue his career elsewhere.

The George Karl Era: Revitalizing the Nuggets

- **New Leadership**: When George Karl took over as head coach in 2005, he brought a fresh perspective to the Denver Nuggets. Known for his fast-paced style of play and emphasis on team chemistry, Karl quickly revitalized the team's performance on the court.

- **Playoff Success**: Under Karl's leadership, the Nuggets experienced postseason success, making multiple playoff appearances and advancing to the Western Conference Finals in 2009. This marked a significant milestone for a franchise that had struggled in previous years.

- **Legacy**: George Karl's time with the Denver Nuggets left a lasting impact on both players and fans alike. His ability to cultivate talent and foster a winning culture set a new standard for the organization, paving the way for future success.

The Rise of Nikola Jokic: A New Era of Nuggets Basketball

- **Emergence of a Star:**

  - In recent years, the Denver Nuggets have witnessed the meteoric rise of center Nikola Jokic.

  - His unique skill set and on-court vision have revolutionized the team's style of play.

- **All-Star Performance:**

  - Jokic's stellar performances have earned him multiple All-Star selections.

  - He has become the focal point of the Nuggets' offense, consistently putting up impressive numbers in points, rebounds, and assists.

- **Playoff Success:**

  - Under Jokic's leadership, the Nuggets have made deep playoff runs, showcasing his ability to elevate his game when it matters most.

  - Fans and analysts alike are optimistic about what the future holds for Jokic and the Denver Nuggets as they strive for championship glory.

Mile High Magic: Memorable Moments in Nuggets History

● **1984 Draft Day Trade:** The Denver Nuggets made a bold move on draft day in 1984, acquiring the rights to Georgetown University standout point guard, John "Hot Rod" Williams. This trade set the stage for one of the most successful eras in franchise history.

● **2009 Playoff Run:** In 2009, led by star player Carmelo Anthony, the Denver Nuggets embarked on a memorable playoff run. They defeated both the New Orleans Hornets and Dallas Mavericks before falling to the Los Angeles Lakers in the Western Conference Finals. Despite not winning it all, this deep playoff run solidified their status as a competitive team in the NBA.

● **2016 'Miracle at Pepsi Center':** The unforgettable game between the Denver Nuggets and Oklahoma City Thunder took place on February 1st, 2016 at Pepsi Center. Down by double digits with less than three minutes left on the clock, miraculous shooting performances from Jamal Murray and Nikola Jokic led to an unprecedented comeback victory for the Nuggets. This moment will forever be etched into Denver Nuggets folklore as one of their greatest comebacks of all time.

From the Pepsi Center to Ball Arena: The Nuggets' Home Court Advantage

The Denver Nuggets have called different arenas home throughout their history. Originally playing at the Denver Auditorium Arena, the team moved to the McNichols Sports Arena in 1975. However, it wasn't until they made the Pepsi Center their home in 1999 that they truly experienced a sense of home court advantage.

1. **Pepsi Center:** The state-of-the-art Pepsi Center became synonymous with Denver basketball success. Fans filled the arena to cheer on their team, creating an intimidating atmosphere for visiting opponents.
2. **Ball Arena:** In 2020, times changed with a new name and logo for the arena now known as Ball Arena. Despite this change, one thing remained constant – the support from loyal fans lifting up the Nuggets during each game.

With a rich history tied to various venues, the Denver Nuggets continue to thrive on their home court advantage at Ball Arena, showcasing their Mile High legacy through every game played on familiar ground.

The Denver Nuggets' Rivalries: Battles on the Court

The Denver Nuggets have faced fierce competition in the NBA, leading to intense rivalries over the years. One of their most notable rivals is the Utah Jazz, with whom they have squared off multiple times in heated matchups. These games always bring out the best in both teams and keep fans on the edge of their seats.

Another long-standing rivalry for the Nuggets is against the Portland Trail Blazers. The battles between these two teams have been legendary, with each game filled with intensity and drama. Whether it's a regular-season showdown or a playoff series, you can always expect an exciting matchup when these two teams face off on the court.

In recent years, another emerging rivalry for the Denver Nuggets has been with the Los Angeles Lakers. As two powerhouse teams in the Western Conference, every meeting between them is highly anticipated by fans and players alike. These games often come down to the wire and showcase some of the best talent in professional basketball today.

The Nuggets' Hall of Famers: Legends of Denver Basketball

- **Alex English**: A scoring machine and one of the greatest offensive players in NBA history, Alex English spent the majority of his career with the Denver Nuggets. Known for his smooth shooting stroke and ability to score from anywhere on the court, English was a fan favorite during his time in Denver. He was inducted into the Naismith Memorial Basketball Hall of Fame in 1997.

- **Dan Issel**: A versatile big man who could score both inside and outside, Dan Issel was a dominant force for the Nuggets in both the ABA and NBA. He ranks as one of the franchise's all-time leading scorers and rebounders. Issel's impact on basketball in Denver cannot be overstated, as he helped establish a winning culture for the team.

- **David Thompson**: Nicknamed "Skywalker" for his incredible leaping ability, David Thompson was a high-flying superstar for the Nuggets in the 1970s. His athleticism and scoring prowess made him one of the most exciting players to watch during his era. Thompson's impact on Denver basketball is still felt today, as he remains one of the most iconic figures in franchise history.

The Evolution of the Nuggets' Logo and Uniforms

Since their inception in 1967, the Denver Nuggets have undergone numerous logo and uniform changes to reflect the team's evolution. The original logo featured a stylized miner with a pickaxe, paying homage to Colorado's rich mining history. In 1974, the team introduced their iconic "rainbow skyline" uniforms, which became synonymous with the franchise during its most successful years in the 1980s.

In recent years, the Nuggets have transitioned to a more modern look with cleaner lines and bold colors. The current primary logo features a gold pickaxe crossed over a basketball on top of a navy blue mountain peak, symbolizing both the team's past and present identity. The uniforms have also evolved to incorporate elements of Denver's mountainous landscape while maintaining ties to their traditional color scheme of powder blue, navy blue, and gold.

Mile High Mentality: The Nuggets' Fanbase

- **Passionate:** The Denver Nuggets' fanbase is known for their unwavering passion and loyalty towards the team. Fans in the Mile High City show up game after game, cheering loudly and proudly for their beloved team.

- **Resilient:** Despite facing ups and downs throughout the years, the Nuggets' fanbase has remained resilient. They continue to support their team through thick and thin, always believing in their ability to overcome challenges and achieve success.

- **Family:** At its core, the Nuggets' fanbase feels like a tight-knit family. Whether celebrating victories or commiserating losses, fans come together to share in the emotions that come with being a part of this dedicated community.

Nuggets in the Community: Making a Difference Off the Court

Community Impact

Off the court, the Denver Nuggets have been actively involved in making a positive impact on their community. Through various initiatives and partnerships, the team has shown a commitment to giving back and supporting those in need. From hosting basketball camps for underprivileged youth to participating in charitable events, the Nuggets have demonstrated that they care deeply about making a difference beyond just winning games.

Charitable Contributions

The Nuggets Foundation, the charitable arm of the organization, plays a key role in supporting local nonprofits and community organizations. Through fundraising efforts and donations, the foundation is able to provide assistance to those facing adversity in the Denver area. Whether it's promoting education, health and wellness programs, or social justice initiatives, the Nuggets are dedicated to being a force for good in their community.

Player Involvement

Many players on the Denver Nuggets roster also take an active role in giving back. Through personal foundations and outreach programs, these athletes use their platform to make a positive impact on society. Whether it's visiting hospitals to spend time with patients or advocating for social causes, these players are committed to using their influence for good both on and off the court.

The Denver Nuggets' Coaching Legacy: Leaders on the Sidelines

- **Early Years**: In their formative years, the Denver Nuggets saw several coaching changes as they navigated through the challenges of building a competitive team in the NBA. Despite early struggles, coaches like Larry Brown and Doug Moe laid the foundation for success by instilling a fast-paced style of play that became synonymous with the franchise.

- **George Karl Era**: George Karl took over as head coach in 2005 and led the Nuggets to multiple playoff appearances during his tenure. Known for his innovative strategies and player development skills, Karl left a lasting impact on the team and helped elevate them to new heights in the Western Conference.

- **Current Leadership**: Under current head coach Michael Malone, the Denver Nuggets have continued to excel on both ends of the court. Malone's emphasis on defense and team chemistry has solidified their status as contenders in a tough Western Conference, keeping alive the legacy of strong leadership on the sidelines for this historic franchise.

The Denver Nuggets' Front Office: Building a Winning Team

The success of the Denver Nuggets can be attributed to their astute front office decisions.

1. **Strong Leadership**: Under the guidance of savvy executives like Tim Connelly, the team has built a roster that is competitive year after year.
2. **Strategic Draft Picks**: The Nuggets have made shrewd draft selections, bringing in key players like Nikola Jokic and Jamal Murray who have become integral to the team's success.
3. **Smart Trades and Free Agent Signings**: By making calculated trades and signings, the front office has been able to acquire talent that fits seamlessly into their system.

Overall, the Denver Nuggets' front office has played a pivotal role in shaping the team into a perennial playoff contender. Their dedication to building a strong roster through smart decision-making has solidified their place as one of the top teams in the NBA.

Mile High Success: Playoff Runs and Challenges

- The Denver Nuggets have a rich history of success in the NBA playoffs, with multiple deep runs showcasing their talent and determination.

- Despite facing tough challenges along the way, including injuries and fierce competition, the Nuggets have continued to persevere and make their mark on the league.

- From memorable playoff series wins to heartbreaking losses, each postseason journey has only added to the legacy of the Denver Nuggets as a competitive and resilient team.

The Nuggets' International Impact: Players from Around the Globe

- Since its inception, the Denver Nuggets have welcomed players from around the globe to their roster.

- These international athletes have not only added diversity to the team but have also made significant contributions on the court.

- From European stars like Nikola Jokic and Danilo Gallinari to African talents like Serge Ibaka and Emmanuel Mudiay, the Nuggets have truly embraced a global approach to building their team.

Embracing Diversity for Success

- By recognizing talent beyond American borders, the Denver Nuggets have been able to create a dynamic and competitive team.

- International players bring unique skills and perspectives that add depth and versatility to the roster.

- This emphasis on diversity has allowed the Nuggets to compete at a high level in an increasingly globalized NBA.

Looking Towards the Future

- As basketball continues to grow in popularity worldwide, we can expect more international players to make their mark on teams like Denver's.

- The Nuggets' commitment to embracing diverse talent bodes well for their future success both domestically and internationally.

Looking to the Future: The Next Chapter for the Denver Nuggets

- The Denver Nuggets are poised for success in the upcoming seasons as they continue to build a talented roster and develop young players.

- With stars like Nikola Jokic leading the way, the team is positioning itself as a contender in the competitive Western Conference.

- Fans can expect thrilling games and exciting playoff runs as the Nuggets look to solidify their place among the NBA's elite teams.

Unforgettable Moments: Revisiting the Denver Nuggets' Thrilling Games and Championship Appearances

The Denver Nuggets have a storied history filled with unforgettable moments that have captivated basketball fans worldwide. From thrilling games to championship appearances, the team has left an indelible mark on the NBA landscape. In this article, we will take a trip down memory lane and revisit some of the most memorable moments in Nuggets' history. Join us as we relive the excitement and drama of their journey to greatness, highlighting key games and pivotal moments that have solidified their place in basketball lore. Get ready to immerse yourself in the rich tapestry of Denver Nuggets' legacy as we delve into their triumphs and heartbreaks on the road to glory.

The Birth of the Denver Nuggets: A Look Back at the Early Years

- **Formation and Entry into NBA**: The Denver Nuggets, originally founded as the Denver Larks in 1967, joined the American Basketball Association (ABA) in 1967 before moving to the National Basketball Association (NBA) in 1976. This transition marked the beginning of a new era for the team.

- **Early Struggles and Promising Players**: In their initial years in the NBA, the Denver Nuggets faced challenges as they adjusted to the competitive nature of the league. However, with star players like Byron Beck and Dan Issel on board, they began to make a name for themselves on both local and national levels.

- **Foundation for Success**: Despite early setbacks, these formative years laid a strong foundation that would eventually lead to memorable moments and thrilling games for fans to enjoy throughout its history. The determination and resilience displayed by the team during this period set them on a path towards future success that would define their legacy in basketball history.

The Nuggets' First Taste of Success: A Trip to the ABA Finals

In the 1975-76 season, the Denver Nuggets made a historic run to the ABA Finals for the first time in franchise history. Led by coach Larry Brown and star player David Thompson, the team captivated fans with their high-flying style of play.

Despite falling short in the finals against Julius Erving's New York Nets, this playoff appearance marked a turning point for the Nuggets and set the stage for future success in the NBA. The energy and excitement surrounding this momentous occasion still resonate with fans today as one of the unforgettable chapters in Nuggets history.

Key highlights:

- Coach Larry Brown's strategic guidance

- Star player David Thompson's electrifying performances

- Impact on setting up future success in NBA

From ABA to NBA: The Nuggets' Transition to the Big League

• In 1976, the Denver Nuggets made the leap from the American Basketball Association (ABA) to join the National Basketball Association (NBA), marking a significant milestone in their history. This move brought new challenges and opportunities for the team as they entered a more competitive league.

• Led by legendary coach Larry Brown, the Nuggets quickly established themselves as a force to be reckoned with in the NBA. They showcased their talent and determination on the court, earning respect from fans and opponents alike. Despite facing tough competition, the Nuggets never backed down, proving that they belonged among basketball's elite.

• The transition from ABA to NBA was not without its struggles, but it ultimately paved the way for future success for the Denver Nuggets. With a rich history filled with memorable moments and thrilling games, this period marked an important chapter in shaping the identity of one of basketball's most beloved teams.

The Arrival of Alex English: A Turning Point in Nuggets History

- In the early 1980s, the Denver Nuggets experienced a significant turning point with the arrival of Alex English.

- English's exceptional scoring ability and leadership skills revitalized the team and captured the hearts of fans across the city.

- His impact on and off the court helped elevate the Nuggets to new heights within the NBA landscape.

With Alex English leading the charge, the Denver Nuggets went on to achieve some of their most memorable moments in franchise history.

The Run-and-Gun Era: How the Nuggets Revolutionized Basketball

During the "Run-and-Gun" era, the Denver Nuggets became known for their fast-paced style of play that revolutionized basketball. They were quick, agile, and always on the move - making them a force to be reckoned with on the court.

Key players like Alex English and Kiki Vandeweghe led the charge, showcasing their scoring prowess and helping usher in a new era of high-scoring games. Their electrifying performances captivated fans and cemented the Nuggets' legacy as trailblazers in modern basketball tactics.

With their up-tempo style and innovative approach to offense, the Nuggets left an indelible mark on the sport, inspiring future generations of players and coaches to push boundaries and embrace change.

The 1994 Playoff Run: Revisiting the Nuggets' Cinderella Story

- In 1994, the Denver Nuggets defied all odds and captured the hearts of basketball fans everywhere with their improbable playoff run.

- Led by legendary coach Dan Issel, along with star players like Dikembe Mutombo and LaPhonso Ellis, the Nuggets were a team on a mission.

- Despite being heavy underdogs in every series they played, the Nuggets managed to upset powerhouse teams like the Seattle SuperSonics and Utah Jazz.

This unforgettable journey culminated in an epic showdown against the eventual champion Houston Rockets. The Nuggets may not have brought home the championship that year, but their inspiring performance will forever be etched in basketball history as one of the greatest Cinderella stories of all time.

The Carmelo Anthony Era: A New Hope for Nuggets Fans

- In the early 2000s, the Denver Nuggets found a new sense of hope and excitement with the arrival of Carmelo Anthony.

- Anthony brought his scoring prowess and leadership to the team, instantly making an impact on the court.

- Under his guidance, the Nuggets achieved playoff success and reached new heights in their pursuit of an NBA championship.

With Carmelo Anthony leading the way, fans had something to cheer about as they witnessed thrilling games and unforgettable moments unfold before their eyes.

The 2009 Western Conference Finals: A Thrilling Showdown with the Lakers

• Denver Nuggets faced a formidable opponent in the Los Angeles Lakers during the 2009 Western Conference Finals.

• The series was filled with intense back-and-forth action, keeping fans on the edge of their seats.

• Despite putting up a valiant effort, the Nuggets fell short as the Lakers ultimately advanced to the NBA Finals.

The matchups between Kobe Bryant and Carmelo Anthony were highlights of the series, showcasing two of the league's top talents. Both teams fought tooth and nail for every basket, making each game a must-watch event. While the outcome wasn't what Nuggets fans had hoped for, the team's performance in this playoff run will always be remembered as a thrilling chapter in franchise history.

The Emergence of Nikola Jokic: The Nuggets' Modern-Day Superstar

- In recent years, Nikola Jokic has solidified himself as the cornerstone of the Denver Nuggets' roster.

- Known for his unique combination of size, passing ability, and basketball IQ, Jokic has evolved into a modern-day superstar.

- His impact on the court goes beyond statistics, as he consistently elevates his teammates with his unselfish style of play.

A Breakout Performance

- One unforgettable moment that highlighted Jokic's talent was during a crucial playoff game where he recorded a triple-double to lead the Nuggets to victory.

- Fans witnessed firsthand how Jokic took control of the game with his scoring, rebounding, and playmaking skills.

- This breakout performance not only showcased his individual brilliance but also encapsulated his importance to the team's success.

The 2020 Playoff Bubble: The Nuggets' Unforgettable Comeback

- In the unprecedented circumstances of the 2020 NBA playoff bubble, the Denver Nuggets faced incredible adversity.

- Down 3-1 in their series against the Utah Jazz, many counted them out – but the Nuggets had other plans.

- Led by Jamal Murray and Nikola Jokic, they clawed their way back with grit and determination.

Their unforgettable comeback captivated fans and showcased the resilience of this young team. With each game, they grew stronger and more confident. Eventually, they made history by becoming only the 12th team in NBA playoff history to come back from a 3-1 deficit. This remarkable feat solidified their place as true contenders in the league and left a lasting impression on basketball fans worldwide.

The Mile High Miracle: A Historic Game 7 Victory

- In a nail-biting showdown, the Denver Nuggets secured a historic Game 7 victory that left fans on the edge of their seats.

- With clutch performances and sheer determination, the Nuggets overcame all odds to emerge triumphant in this unforgettable game.

- This thrilling victory will forever be etched in the memories of fans and players alike, showcasing the resilience and unwavering spirit of the Denver Nuggets.

An Epic Battle Against All Odds

- Facing formidable opponents, the Denver Nuggets fought tooth and nail in a battle that will go down in history as one for the ages.

- Every basket made, every defensive stop executed was crucial in securing this monumental win for the team.

- From heart-stopping moments to jubilant celebrations, this Game 7 victory epitomized everything that makes basketball such an exhilarating sport.

A Moment of Glory for Denver

- As the final buzzer sounded and confetti rained down from above, the Denver Nuggets savored a well-deserved moment of glory after an epic Game 7 triumph.

- The players' dedication and teamwork paid off in this historic victory that solidified their place in basketball lore.

● This unforgettable milestone will forever hold a special place in the hearts of both fans and players as they relive the magic of that night at "The Mile High" arena.

The 1985 Western Conference Semifinals: A Classic Showdown with the Lakers

● In 1985, the Denver Nuggets faced off against the mighty Los Angeles Lakers in a thrilling Western Conference Semifinals series.

● Led by star players like Alex English and Fat Lever, the Nuggets put up a valiant fight against Magic Johnson and Kareem Abdul-Jabbar.

● Despite their best efforts, the Nuggets ultimately fell short in a hard-fought series that went to seven games.

The matchup between the Nuggets and Lakers in the 1985 Western Conference Semifinals will always be remembered as a classic showdown between two talented teams. The intensity of each game and the back-and-forth action kept fans on the edge of their seats throughout the series. While the Nuggets ultimately did not advance to the next round, their performance against one of the NBA's best teams solidified their reputation as a competitive force to be reckoned with in years to come.

The Nuggets' First Division Title: A Milestone Achievement

In a historic season, the Denver Nuggets clinched their first division title, marking a significant milestone in the franchise's history. This achievement was the culmination of years of hard work, dedication, and perseverance by players and coaching staff alike.

Key moments in this remarkable journey included standout performances from star players like Nikola Jokic and Jamal Murray, as well as strategic decisions made by head coach Michael Malone. The team's unity and determination were on full display throughout the season, leading them to victory in the fiercely competitive Western Conference.

The 1988 All-Star Game: Denver Shines on the National Stage

- In 1988, the city of Denver hosted the NBA All-Star Game, bringing together basketball's biggest stars for a showcase of talent.

- Fans packed into McNichols Sports Arena to witness legends like Larry Bird and Magic Johnson compete in an electrifying game.

- The atmosphere was electric as the best players in the league showcased their skills and entertained fans with high-flying dunks and clutch shots.

The 1988 All-Star Game put Denver on the map as a premier destination for basketball events, highlighting the passion of its fans and the excitement of its vibrant sports scene.

The 1976 ABA Championship: The Nuggets' Crowning Achievement

• In 1976, the Denver Nuggets claimed their first and only ABA Championship in a thrilling series against the New York Nets.

• Led by head coach Larry Brown and star player David Thompson, the Nuggets showcased a combination of tenacity and skill that proved unstoppable.

• This championship victory solidified the Nuggets' place in basketball history and remains a cherished moment for fans to this day.

The resilience displayed by the team during critical moments in the playoffs was nothing short of inspiring. From buzzer-beater shots to dominant defensive plays, every member of the roster contributed their part towards this historic win. As they hoisted the championship trophy high above their heads, it marked a culmination of years of hard work, dedication, and belief in each other's abilities. In that unforgettable moment, Denver etched its name among basketball legends with an indelible mark of glory.

The 2006 Dunk Contest: Revisiting JR Smith's Iconic Performance

- In the 2006 NBA Slam Dunk Contest, JR Smith wowed fans and judges alike with his incredible athleticism and creativity.

- Smith's dunks were a sight to behold, showcasing his raw talent and fearless approach to the competition.

- From his between-the-legs dunk to his off-the-backboard alley-oop finish, Smith left an indelible mark on the contest.

Smith's performance in the 2006 Dunk Contest not only solidified his status as one of the league's top high-flyers but also provided Nuggets fans with a moment they would never forget. His show-stopping display of skill and flair captivated audiences around the world and remains etched in basketball history. While he may not have taken home the trophy that night, JR Smith undoubtedly won over countless admirers with his unforgettable performance.

The 2013 Playoff Series vs the Warriors: A Clash of Styles

The Denver Nuggets faced off against the Golden State Warriors in a thrilling playoff series in 2013. The Nuggets, known for their fast-paced style of play and high-scoring offense, clashed with the Warriors' sharpshooting lineup led by Stephen Curry.

1. **Run-and-Gun vs Outside Shooting:** The series showcased a contrast in playing styles, with the Nuggets pushing the pace and attacking the paint while the Warriors relied on their three-point shooting to spread the floor and create scoring opportunities.
2. **Intensity and Physicality:** Both teams brought a level of intensity to each game, resulting in hard-fought battles on both ends of the court. The physical play added an extra layer of excitement for fans watching at home and in the arena.

In conclusion, this playoff series between two contrasting styles provided basketball fans with unforgettable moments that showcased both teams' strengths and weaknesses as they battled it out for supremacy on the court.

The Nuggets' Hall of Famers: Celebrating Denver's Basketball Legends

The Nuggets' Hall of Famers

1. **David Thompson**: A scoring machine known for his high-flying dunks and incredible athleticism, David Thompson was a key player in the Denver Nuggets' history. Inducted into the Basketball Hall of Fame in 1996, Thompson's impact on the team is still felt today.

2. **Alex English**: With silky-smooth moves and a deadly jump shot, Alex English remains one of the most beloved players in Nuggets history. Inducted into the Hall of Fame in 1997, English's scoring prowess and leadership were instrumental in shaping the franchise.

3. **Dikembe Mutombo**: Known for his dominant defense and iconic finger wag, Dikembe Mutombo brought intensity and toughness to the court for the Denver Nuggets. Inducted into the Hall of Fame in 2015, Mutombo's presence as a rim protector was unmatched during his time with the team.

The Rocky Mountain Rivalry: Nuggets vs Jazz

• The Denver Nuggets and the Utah Jazz have a long-standing rivalry in the NBA's Western Conference, known for their intense matchups and close games.

• One of the most memorable moments between these two teams was during the 2010 playoffs when they faced off in a thrilling first-round series.

• In Game 4, Carmelo Anthony scored an impressive buzzer-beater to secure a crucial win for the Nuggets, adding to the excitement of this fierce rivalry.

Overall, whenever these two teams meet on the court, fans can expect nothing less than heart-pounding action and unforgettable moments.

The Nuggets' Future: A Bright Outlook for Denver's Basketball Team

• **Young Talent**: With a roster full of promising young players like Jamal Murray and Michael Porter Jr., the Nuggets have a strong foundation for future success.

• **Experienced Leadership**: Coach Michael Malone has proven himself to be a skilled leader, guiding the team to multiple playoff appearances and instilling a winning mentality in his players.

• **Community Support**: The city of Denver has shown unwavering support for their basketball team, creating an exciting atmosphere at every home game that motivates the players to perform at their best.

In conclusion, the Denver Nuggets have all the key elements in place to continue their journey towards championship contention in the coming years.

The Legends of the Denver Nuggets: Iconic Players, Coaches, and Unforgettable Fan Moments

The Denver Nuggets have a storied history filled with iconic players, legendary coaches, and unforgettable fan moments that have solidified their place in NBA folklore. From the gritty play of Alex English to the powerhouse presence of Carmelo Anthony, the Nuggets have been home to some of the most talented athletes in basketball history. Coaches like Doug Moe and George Karl have left an indelible mark on the team's legacy, guiding them through both triumphs and challenges. And let's not forget about the passionate fans who fill the Pepsi Center night after night, creating an electric atmosphere that can't be matched. Join us as we delve into the legends of the Denver Nuggets and explore how they've shaped one of the NBA's most beloved franchises.

Alex English: The Franchise Player

• Alex English remains a pivotal figure in the history of the Denver Nuggets.

• Known for his scoring prowess and smooth playing style, English solidified himself as the franchise player during his time with the team.

• He consistently led the Nuggets in points per game and was named to multiple All-Star teams.

During his tenure with the Nuggets,

• English became the highest scorer in team history

• His impact on and off the court earned him respect from fans and teammates alike.

Carmelo Anthony: A Denver Legend

● Carmelo Anthony made a significant impact during his time with the Denver Nuggets.

● Known for his scoring prowess and clutch performances, he became a fan favorite.

● Anthony led the Nuggets to multiple playoff appearances and was a key player in shaping the team's identity.

Legacy in Denver

● His scoring ability and leadership on and off the court left a lasting legacy in Denver.

● Despite eventually leaving the Nuggets, Carmelo Anthony remains one of the most beloved players in franchise history.

● His impact continues to be felt by fans who fondly remember his time wearing a Nuggets jersey.

Dikembe Mutombo: Defensive Dominance

• Standing tall at 7 feet 2 inches, Dikembe Mutombo was a force to be reckoned with on the defensive end.

• Known for his shot-blocking prowess, Mutombo's iconic finger wag after blocking shots struck fear into opponents.

• A four-time Defensive Player of the Year, he anchored the Denver Nuggets defense during his time with the team.

Legacy and Impact

• Mutombo's legacy lives on in his countless blocked shots and unforgettable moments on the court.

• His impact extended beyond basketball as well, with humanitarian efforts in Africa earning him global recognition.

• The Hall of Famer remains a beloved figure among Denver Nuggets fans for his contributions to the team and community.

Chauncey Billups: The Steady Leader

1. **NBA Champion**: Known for his leadership on and off the court, Chauncey Billups guided the Denver Nuggets to their first Western Conference Finals appearance in 2009.
2. **Clutch Performer**: Nicknamed "Mr. Big Shot," Billups thrived under pressure situations, making crucial plays when it mattered most.
3. **Respected Veteran**: With a calm demeanor and high basketball IQ, Billups quickly earned the respect of teammates, coaches, and fans alike.

Chauncey Billups' impact on the Denver Nuggets transcended statistics; his presence elevated the team's performance and instilled a winning culture that reverberated throughout the organization. He remains a beloved figure in Nuggets history, symbolizing resilience and excellence both on and off the court.

Nikola Jokic: The Joker's Reign

- Nikola Jokic, affectionately known as "The Joker," has solidified his place as one of the most dominant players in Denver Nuggets history.

- With his unique skillset as a versatile big man who can score, pass, and rebound with exceptional efficiency, Jokic has captured the hearts of Nuggets fans around the world.

- From winning NBA MVP honors to leading the team deep into the playoffs, Jokic's impact on the court is undeniable.

The All-Star Center's Legacy

- As an integral part of the Denver Nuggets organization, Nikola Jokic has set numerous records and achieved milestones that will forever be etched in franchise history.

- His charismatic personality and humble demeanor have endeared him to fans both on and off the court, making him a true fan favorite.

- Whether it's his pinpoint passes or clutch shot-making ability, Jokic's reign as "The Joker" continues to leave a lasting legacy in Nuggets lore.

David Thompson: Skywalking to Success

• **Peak Performance:** David Thompson, known as "Skywalker," soared above the competition during his time with the Denver Nuggets.

• **Scoring Sensation:** Thompson's explosive scoring abilities made him a fan favorite and a force to be reckoned with on the court.

• **Legacy of Greatness:** His impact on the Nuggets franchise is still felt today, cementing his place as one of the iconic players in team history.

Dan Issel: The Mile High Scoring Machine

Dan Issel was a driving force for the Denver Nuggets during his time with the team. Known as "The Horse", he was a prolific scorer who could dominate games with his scoring prowess. Issel's ability to score in a variety of ways made him a nightmare for opposing defenses.

- **Prolific Scorer**: Dan Issel consistently put up impressive numbers, averaging over 20 points per game in each of his seasons with the Nuggets.

- **Versatile Offense**: His inside-outside game allowed him to score from anywhere on the court, making him a difficult matchup for any defender.

- **Legendary Status**: To this day, Dan Issel remains one of the most iconic players in Denver Nuggets history, solidifying his place as an unforgettable legend in Mile High City sports lore.

Fat Lever: The Versatile Guard

● Fat Lever, a key player for the Denver Nuggets in the 1980s, was known for his versatility on the court.

● As a guard, Lever possessed exceptional skills in scoring, rebounding, and playmaking.

● Lever's ability to fill up stat sheets with points, assists, and rebounds made him a valuable asset to the Nuggets.

During his time with the team:

● Lever led the Nuggets to multiple playoff appearances.

● His leadership and all-around talent endeared him to fans and teammates alike.

● To this day, Fat Lever remains an iconic figure in Denver Nuggets history.

Doug Moe: The Mastermind Coach

Doug Moe, known as the mastermind coach of the Denver Nuggets, led the team with his innovative strategies and high-paced offense. His coaching style revolutionized the game and left a lasting impact on basketball history.

- Renowned for his unorthodox methods

- Emphasized teamwork and ball movement

- Coached Nuggets to multiple playoff appearances

Moe's colorful personality and dedication to developing young talent made him a beloved figure in Denver sports. His legacy continues to inspire coaches and players alike in the NBA.

George Karl: Leading the Nuggets to Success

George Karl coached the Denver Nuggets from 2005 to 2013, leaving a lasting impact on the team and its fans. His strategic coaching style propelled the Nuggets to numerous successful seasons during his tenure.

- Under Karl's leadership, the Nuggets made it to the playoffs every year he was head coach.

- Known for his defensive emphasis and fast-paced offense, Karl brought out the best in players like Carmelo Anthony and Chauncey Billups.

Karl's time with the Denver Nuggets cemented his legacy as one of the most successful coaches in franchise history.

Michael Adams: The Three-Point Specialist

Michael Adams made a lasting impact on the Denver Nuggets as a three-point specialist. His precision shooting and quick release kept defenders on their toes throughout his career with the team.

- Known for his ability to stretch the floor and drain long-range shots

- Played with passion and determination every game

- Became a fan favorite for his electrifying style of play

Fans still remember Michael Adams as one of the iconic players who brought excitement to the court during his time with the Denver Nuggets.

Kiki Vandeweghe: The Sharpshooter

Known for his deadly jump shot and smooth scoring ability, Kiki Vandeweghe became a household name during his time with the Denver Nuggets. His precise shooting touch made him a threat from anywhere on the court, earning him respect as one of the league's top sharpshooters.

● Vandeweghe's offensive prowess helped elevate the Nuggets to new heights, leading them to multiple playoff appearances and thrilling fans with his scoring outbursts.

● With an impressive career average of over 20 points per game, Vandeweghe solidified himself as a key player in Nuggets history and left a lasting impact on the franchise.

Vandeweghe's legacy lives on through his contributions to Denver basketball, showcasing what it means to be a true sharpshooter in every sense of the word.

Allen Iverson: The Answer in Denver

• As one of the most iconic players in NBA history, **Allen Iverson** made a significant impact during his time with the Denver Nuggets.

• Known for his electrifying style of play and fearless attitude on the court, Iverson quickly won over fans with his scoring prowess and competitive spirit.

• Despite a short tenure in Denver, Iverson's legacy as a Nugget is still remembered fondly by both fans and teammates alike.

Jamal Murray: The Young Star Rising

Jamal Murray, a rising star in the NBA, has quickly made a name for himself as one of the Denver Nuggets' most promising players. With his impressive scoring ability and clutch performances, Murray has proven to be a key player for the team.

- Known for his smooth shooting stroke and fearless demeanor on the court

- Has already set numerous records in his young career

- Continues to improve each season, showcasing his dedication to becoming an elite player in the league

Jusuf Nurkic: The Bosnian Beast

- Standing at 7 feet tall, Jusuf Nurkic quickly made a name for himself as a dominant force on the court.

- Known for his aggressive playing style and impressive defensive skills, Nurkic earned the nickname "The Bosnian Beast" among fans and teammates alike.

- During his time with the Denver Nuggets, Nurkic's intimidating presence in the paint struck fear into opposing players and helped solidify his reputation as one of the most formidable centers in the league.

Nurkic's impact went beyond just statistics:

- His intensity and passion for the game resonated with fans, making him a beloved figure in Denver.

- Despite facing injuries during his tenure with the Nuggets, Nurkic always displayed resilience and determination, inspiring both his teammates and supporters.

- Even after leaving Denver to continue his career elsewhere, Jusuf Nurkic remains a legendary figure in Nuggets history.

Mutombo's Finger Wag: An Iconic Gesture

During his time with the Denver Nuggets, Dikembe Mutombo became known for his signature move – the finger wag. This iconic gesture involved Mutombo shaking his index finger at opposing players after blocking their shots, a symbol of his defensive prowess and dominance on the court. Fans would erupt in cheers every time Mutombo delivered the finger wag, solidifying its place as one of the most memorable moments in Nuggets history.

The finger wag not only showcased Mutombo's incredible shot-blocking abilities but also added a touch of playfulness to his intimidating presence on the court. It became a rallying cry for Nuggets fans and an enduring symbol of success and excellence in defense. To this day, when people think of Dikembe Mutombo, they can't help but picture him raising that index finger high in the air, forever cementing his legacy as one of Denver's all-time greats.

In summary,

- The finger wag was synonymous with Dikembe Mutombo during his tenure with the Denver Nuggets.

- Fans cheered every time he performed this iconic gesture after blocking shots.

- The move highlighted both his defensive skills and playful demeanor on the court.

The Rainbow Skyline: A Retro Classic

● The Denver Nuggets' iconic "Rainbow Skyline" jerseys from the 1980s are a symbol of nostalgia for fans.

● Featuring vibrant colors and a distinctive design, these jerseys have become collector's items that evoke memories of past glory.

● The retro classic appeal of the "Rainbow Skyline" uniforms continues to endure among basketball enthusiasts.

In the history of NBA fashion, few uniforms stand out as much as the Denver Nuggets' colorful skyline. With its bold hues and unique aesthetic, this jersey has remained an emblematic representation of the team's heritage. As fans don their own versions of these throwback jerseys, they pay homage to a bygone era in Nuggets history when stars like Alex English graced the court.

The Mile High Miracle: Carmelo's Game-Winner

- In a thrilling NBA game against the Dallas Mavericks, Carmelo Anthony delivered a moment that would go down in Denver Nuggets history.

- With just 1. 9 seconds remaining on the clock, Carmelo received an inbound pass and sank a miraculous three-pointer to seal the victory for his team.

- The crowd at the Pepsi Center erupted in cheers as they witnessed one of the most iconic game-winning shots ever seen.

A Legendary Performance

- Carmelo's clutch shot showcased his incredible talent and ability to perform under pressure.

- His leadership on the court during crucial moments solidified his status as one of the greatest players to don a Nuggets jersey.

- This unforgettable moment will forever be etched in the memories of fans who were lucky enough to witness it live.

Rocky the Mountain Lion: The Beloved Mascot

- A fixture at Denver Nuggets games, Rocky the Mountain Lion has become an iconic symbol of the team.

- With his energetic dance moves and entertaining antics, fans young and old are always delighted to see him on the court.

- Whether he's pumping up the crowd or interacting with players, Rocky adds a unique spark to every game.

Rocky embodies the spirit of the team and is beloved by fans for his playful personality. His presence at Nuggets games brings an extra element of fun and excitement that truly enhances the overall fan experience. From kids eagerly awaiting high fives from him to adults cheering on his halftime performances, Rocky has a way of bringing everyone together in support of their favorite team.

The Pepsi Center: Home of the Nuggets' Faithful Fans

• Located in Denver, Colorado, the Pepsi Center serves as the hub for all things Denver Nuggets.

• Despite its name change to Ball Arena, the memories and excitement of fans remain anchored in the history of this iconic basketball venue.

• With a seating capacity of over 19,000, the arena buzzes with energy during every game, creating an electric atmosphere that fuels both players and spectators alike.

From die-hard fans waving their foam fingers to families enjoying a night out at the game, the Pepsi Center embodies unity and passion for basketball. As one enters through its doors, they are enveloped by a sense of community shared among fellow supporters. It's not just a place to watch a game; it's where lifelong memories are made and cherished by generations of loyal followers.

Whether cheering on their favorite player or celebrating victory after a hard-fought match-up, fans at the Pepsi Center form an unbreakable bond with each other and with their beloved team. This shared love for basketball transcends mere spectatorship; it transforms ordinary individuals into an inseparable part of something greater - The Denver Nuggets family.

Don't miss out!

Visit the website below and you can sign up to receive emails whenever Epic History publishes a new book. There's no charge and no obligation.

https://books2read.com/r/B-A-FTVBB-HLHYC

Connecting independent readers to independent writers.

Did you love *Denver Nuggets Epic History*? Then you should read *New Jersey Devils Epic History*[1] by Epic History!

"New Jersey Devils - Epic History" is an enthralling deep dive into the rich tapestry of one of hockey's most fascinating franchises. Perfect for any Devils fan, this book is brimming with trivia, fun facts, and a comprehensive account of the team's journey from its humble beginnings to its status as an NHL powerhouse.

Every page of this captivating volume is a treasure trove for hockey enthusiasts. Discover the lesser-known stories and behind-the-scenes drama that have defined the New Jersey Devils. From nail-biting playoffs to the strategies that secured their Stanley Cups, this book covers it all.

Immerse yourself in the world of the Devils through vivid narratives and anecdotes. Learn about the legendary players and iconic coaches

---

who have shaped the team's history. This book is more than just a recounting of games; it's a celebration of the team's spirit and resilience.

"New Jersey Devils - Epic History" is not only an informative read but also an ideal gift for any sports fan. It's a journey through the milestones and memorable moments that have cemented the Devils' place in NHL lore. With each chapter, you'll uncover a new layer of the team's legacy, making it a perfect addition to any fan's collection.

Whether you're a seasoned supporter or new to the world of hockey, this book promises to enhance your appreciation of the game. It's a testament to the enduring allure of the New Jersey Devils and a must-have for anyone who cherishes the thrill of the sport.

Also by Epic History

New Jersey Devils Epic History
Detroit Red Wings Epic History
Denver Nuggets Epic History

www.ingramcontent.com/pod-product-compliance
Lightning Source LLC
Chambersburg PA
CBHW061619130726
47996CB00003B/1050